GLAD THAT I LIVE AM I

GLAD THAT I LIVE AM I

A Collection of Poems

Helen O. Atkins

Edited with an Introduction by
Melanie Atkins Anderson

IMAGO
PRESS
TUCSON ARIZONA

Published in the United States of America by:

Imago Press
3710 East Edison
Tucson AZ 85716

Library of Congress Control Number: 2015940485

Book and Cover Design by Leila Joiner

Cover and interior photographs © Denrique Preudhomme

ISBN 978-1-935437-95-6
ISBN 1-935437-95-X

Printed in the United States of America on Acid-Free Paper

In memory of my mother,
Helen Irene Ogle Atkins,
teacher and poet
author of this collection

Contents

Introduction

My mother was born Helen Irene Ogle in Ithaca, New York, on February 14, 1908. She lived with her father, older sister, and maternal grandmother. Her mother died when she was but seven months old.

When she was nine years old, her father, a Cornell University graduate and one of the founders of the Alpha Phi Alpha Fraternity, accepted a job on Capitol Hill for Wyoming Senator Francis Warren. Soon after accepting this job, he sent for his two daughters in Ithaca and brought them to live with him and his mother in Washington, DC.

Helen remained in Washington where she married and had two children, received a teaching certificate in Elementary Education from the Minor Normal School, a B.S. in English from Howard University, and taught the third and fourth grades until she retired. Her after-retirement activities included traveling, starting a poetry club, participating in a religious group called Anawin, and of course, writing poetry. She died on December 25, 2009, a few weeks before her 102nd birthday.

Helen had learned to read before she entered school and always loved books and poetry. As an elementary school teacher, she shared this love of poetry with her students and colleagues. She was a profound public speaker and an excellent wordsmith. She was often asked to write plays for her students and to serve as speaker or mistress of ceremonies for all kinds of events including graduations, retirements, anniversaries, and holidays.

This collection of poems was written over the course of her lifetime and reflects her thoughts about the things that mattered to her the most. She used her poetry to express her feelings and to show her deep connection with her family and friends, her religious beliefs, and her spiritual values. She writes of universal themes that touch the heart and soul of everyone who experiences her work.

The book is divided into four sections:

Prayers – demonstrations of her faith and her belief in a higher power

Family – expressions of her love and pride for those that were closest to her

Of This and That – reflections of a miscellaneous array of topics from love and friendship to beauty and nature

Holidays – celebrations of those popular days which she held most dearly

Enjoy!

Melanie Atkins Anderson, daughter

1
Prayers

Lord, You, the Potter

Lord, You the Potter, I the clay
Beautiful in Your image, let me stay!
In the fire of Your love, bend me to Your will
In the hallow of Your hand, hold me still.

Mold me and shape me, keep ever by my side
Jesus, my Saviour, my light and my guide
Pliant, ever remembering, You, Lord, the Potter, I the clay
May Mary be my mother and example, day by day!

At peace, humble, loving
When I'm all that I should be
May Mary, my mother, Jesus, my brother
Bring me safe home, dear Lord, to thee.

A Prayer of Love

Eternal Father as we begin our journey today
In all we speak or hear – in all our eyes behold
In our fun and fellowship along the way
May Thy love our hearts enfold!

For Thou hast tonight Love – a holy word
Vibrant – verdant, ever growing
Faith, Hope, Love the powerful third
From the Blood of the Lamb – ever flowing!

So today and as long as we live
May we garner Love's treasure
Thru the merits of Jesus who did to give
His love, in full, full measure!

Thus in His name we dare to plead
For ourselves and for all we hold dear
For Health, for Safety, Strength to meet each daily need
For the joy of knowing that Love casts out fear!

So with the confident love of the Christian heart
I quote from "Whittier's Eternal Goodness" in part
I know not where His islands lift
Their fronded palms in air
I only know I cannot drift
Beyond His Love and care!

Morning Prayer

Heavenly Father, we thank you for the circle of the day.
Today, and every day we offer for your honor and glory.
Everything we say, everything we do, every meditation of
our hearts
May they be acceptable and pleasing to you.
This we ask in Jesus name. Amen

Author's note:

I once said to one of my daughter's coworkers that trite expression, "Have a good day."

"Oh, no," she answered. "Don't say that, say 'Make yourself a good day.'"

Thereby, she put the responsibility squarely on my shoulders. It was to be *my* words, *my* thoughts, *my* deeds that would make the day. It is so - We read in the Sanskrit – Listen to the Exhortation of the Dawn—Look to this Day! – For it is Life, the very Life of Life. –In its brief course lie all the Verities and Realities of your existence – The Bliss of Growth – The Glory of Action – The Splendor of Beauty! ---- For Yesterday is but a dream. And Tomorrow is only a Vision, But TODAY well-lived makes every Yesterday a dream of Happiness – and every Tomorrow a Vision of Hope. Look well therefore to this day. Such is the Salutation of the Dawn!

Yahweh, My God

Yahweh, You have told us
Behold, I have carved your names in the palms of my hands
I have called *you* by name
Everyone who is named is mine
I love you and I created you for my glory
You are precious in my eyes and
I will do all things for you
Therefore do not be afraid!

For this loving care of us
For the friends here gathered round Thy table, Lord
For the bounty of the earth that provides the food we eat
For love, for family and friends
For *all good* things
For *whatever* You may ask of us
Yahweh, in Joy we offer praise and thanksgiving
And ever Thy name we adore.

Amen

I Went to Look for God

I went to look for God
A tall mountain did I climb
There lifted my eyes to heaven
Searching for my Lord divine.

I plodded through the valley wide
Fragrant with its fruited trees
And waving wind tossed grain
And called out for God to the gentle breeze.

I walked for miles to the ocean shores
And looked into its briny deep.
Again I cried, O Lord, come to me
Abide with me before I sleep.

And then a peace came over me
A healing, all-encompassing calm.
A gentle voice seemed to say
Look within yourself for my healing balm.

I See God

I see God in autumn leaves
In a child's upturned face
In majestic spreading trees
In the beauty of far flung space.

I hear God in winds that blow
In gentle raindrops on the grass
In the voices of people I know
In the footsteps of all who pass.

I feel God in every gentle touch
In each kindly thing done for me
In love that means so very much
In peace, dear God, that comes from knowing Thee!

Let There Be Light

Now God said, Let there be light
And thus he separated day from night
As time went on, God planted in Eden a garden fair
Created Adam and Eve and placed them there
But the woman, Eve, and Adam, her mate
Disobeyed God and thus sealed man's fate.

From then on people walked in sin
With little thought of where they were going – or where they had been
But God, our loving Father, had a plan
To save from sin the willful creature Man.

So he sent Jesus, His Son, to be our very brother
To save us from sin and teach us to love one another
Christ was the Light sent to the Earth
To walk with us and show us our worth
Love was Christ's watchword, Faith was the key
Of the Light he handed to you and to me.

We are the Light of the world, so let us go forth from here
Holding high our torch burning bright and clear
Oh what a privilege for you and me
To shine forth walking hand in hand
Dear Jesus with Thee!

Prayer for the Aged

Lord, Thou knowest that I am growing older.

Keep me from getting too talkative and particularly from the fatal habit of thinking that I must say something on every occasion.

Release me from craving to try to straighten out everyone's affairs.

Keep my mind free from the recital of endless details – give me wings to get to the point.

I ask for grace enough to listen to the details of other's pains. Help me to endure them with patience, but seal my lips to my own aches and pains. They are increasing and my love of rehearsing them is becoming sweeter as the days go by.

Teach me the glorious lesson that occasionally it is possible that I may be mistaken.

Keep me reasonably sweet. I do not want to be a saint, some of them are so hard to live with, but a sour old person is one of the crowning works of the devil.

Make me thoughtful but not bossy.

With all my vast store of wisdom, it seems a pity not to use it all – but Thou knowest Lord, that I want a few friends at the end.

Lord, Guide Me

On My 87th Birthday

On February 14, [1995], Valentine's Day, I was 87 years old. 87 years old is 1,044 months; 4,524 weeks; 31,778 days; 762,120 hours.

Gracious Lord, what treasure
Have I given back to you full measure
For the gifts of time you have given me.
Have I served you generously?
All I can say is that whether
I laughed or cried
Always, dear Lord, you were by my side.
When I fell, you lifted me
When I was blind, you helped me see.
And I have learned I'm not alone ever
For you are my shield, my fortress forever.

I cannot answer what I have done.
But I know what you have done for me.
What I have done I cannot tell
But you, dear Lord, have served me well.

This is the prayer I wrote to guide me
And pray it daily to keep you beside me.

My Daily Prayer

God has been good to me.
There have been and are rough times,
But I bear all as patiently as I can
Secure in the love of Jesus.
How can my heart be troubled with Jesus at my side?
By the wounds he suffered, in the drops of his precious blood shed for me
I know that my Redeemer lived and that as long as I trust and believe, I shall be saved.

In the time left allotted to me, help me Lord.
Let me grow lovely growing old.
There is loveliness in old laces, old silks.
Let me be lovely, too!
Let me be sorry for my sins, not from fear of Hell, but because they are unworthy of the love of God.

As each day ends, forgive me, O Lord, for any unkind
thought, word, or deed, and lift me up when morning comes to carry on.
Safe in the Divine Love.
Blessed Mother, Saints of God, join me in this my daily prayer.

Sometimes the Path Is Lonely

Lord, sometimes the path is lonely
The light seems far, far away
Burdens hang so heavy, Father
And dark and difficult the way.

Often I cannot bear, dear Lord
All the problems that beset me
Yet I know I can depend
Always and forever on Thee!

Lift me up, Heavenly Father
Jesus, take my faltering hand
Holy Spirit, be with me
In this dark and lonely land.

Lead me through Life's tangled maze
Leaning, dear Lord, only on you
Knowing that your guiding love
Will bring me always safely through!

I'm Empty

I'm empty, Lord, depleted
Drained the cup
Sweet, sweet Jesus
Fill it up!

I'm thirsty, Lord, thirsty
For your cooling spring
Wash me, Lord, and to
Your garment, let me cling!

My heart cries out
Dear Lord for Thee, only Thee
Hold me in *your* Heart, Lord
This is my plea!

Come and be with me, Lord
As you always were before
Lift your fallen child, Lord
Plant her feet firmly on the shore!

A Blessing Before Lunch

Two words as used by Jesus- both begin with "A"
And are used by a happy Christian every day
The first is for "Abba," the Father who created you and me
The second for "Amen" or Let it be!

Now the first Amen was said for you and me
By our Godparents and the church community
But later we must say
Our own Amen's as we accept Abba's will and way.

So Abba's love for you in my heart is ringing
And today's Amen's in my heart are singing.

So Amen, Abba, Amen
Amen for evening's starry skies
Amen for sunset and sunrise
Amen for morning tea or coffee
Amen for the summer rain and sun
Amen for flowers that warm the heart of everyone

Amen, Abba, Amen
Amen for signs of love like bread and wine
Amen for friendship – yours and mine
Amen for the beauty of your name
Amen for all of us who came

Amen for pleasure, pain, and caring
Amen for blessing and gracing our table and sharing

My Church

My Catholic faith is dear to me
It embraces all my love
In the arms of my dear church
I know that God is love.

At her altar when I kneel
Mary, my mother, looks down on me
A warm safe feeling steals into my heart
For it is she, dear Jesus, who keeps me close to Thee.

There at holy mass, I live
On Calvary, with Mary's son, Christ the King
And with priest and faithful I become
A part of His dear suffering.

Blessed church within thy walls
(For saint and sinner along life's road)
Is all I'll ever need or want
By God's grace, thru Thee, on me bestowed.

Holy, Catholic, Apostolic, One
Four marks my Jesus gave to Thee
From them and in them my church
With grace, leads me to eternity.

When I walk the way of the cross
Humble, sorrowful, penitent
I learn the lesson of sacrifice
That my life may be better – more content.

A Blessing for Little Children

Little children live near and far
In other lands than this
No matter where they are
They love their mother's kiss.

At night when my prayers I say
I'll ask my Jesus them to bless
Whether they live here or far away.

I Think of Jesus: A Children's Prayer

I think of Jesus when I say
My grace before each meal
I thank you, Lord, this day
Thank you for the food I eat.

I think of Jesus when at night
I lay me down to sleep
Watch me, Lord, 'til morning bright
In His care I keep.

I think of Jesus when I rise
From my little bed in early day
For He is kind and good and wise
He'll care for me as I play.

Love One Another

You are loved
As Christ told us to love
As brothers and sisters
With Him.

Our love is less perfect than His
But we try.
We stumble.
We fall.
With His help
We rise and try again.
For He has told us
To love one another
Even as He loved us.

Some are easy to love
Like you
Because you are God's child
And walk His way.
Some are hard to love
But they, too, are God's children.

And maybe the fault is ours
But still we try
To keep His love
Ever burning like a flame
Until He calls us to eternal love.

Because He told us to
Reach out and touch
One another with Love
I give you my love.

A New Page

Oh God, here is a new day
A gift from you
Thank you, lord
I will unwrap your gift with joy.

What is it, Lord?
Let me see.
Ah, it is a fresh unblemished page.
It looks as if it was fashioned with threads
From His robe
And on the top, it says "today."

What else is this in the box?
A pen with my picture on it
And my name, and the word "write"
A card is in the gift
It says, "Everyday
A new page will be given to you
Clear, unblemished
And I will take away the old."

What a gift, Lord.

Who Am I?

Who am I?
  Earthling
  Changeling
  Lucifer's child
  Or God's
Do I know who I am?
Yea, Lord, I am God's child, created in His image.

Where am I going?
  To insure the status quo
  To blaze new trails
  To discover new worlds
  To catch a falling star
  To conquer the universe
  To seek God
Do I know where I am going?
Yea, Lord, I am going to seek a closer walk with Thee.

How am I going?
  Rushing like the wind
  Running like the horse
  Panting up the mountain
  Struggling in deep waters
  Listening to my Lord speak to me
Do we know how we are going?
Yes, Lord, you will tell us. Speak. We are listening.

Why am I going?
  To join the fray
  To gain notoriety
  To get rid of my problems
  To seek the kingdom of God
  To discover God within me
Do I know why I am going?

Yea, Lord, we seek first the kingdom of God within us to help guide.

When am I going?
    Tomorrow (or next day)
    In the bye and bye
    This evening
    Now
Do I know when I am going?
Yea, Lord, Give us this day.

Dilemma

A light blows in my heart
Of faith and love, it is a part
But can that light lead the way
To the dawn of Heaven's beauteous day?
Or is there another, brighter light
To lead the way from the paths of night?

I seek, dear God, I seek to come to Thee
In the way Thou meant, O Lord, to be
The straight and narrow way, Thy chosen one
Open that gate that Thy will may be done.

So I bow my knee and pray
For guidance along the bitter way
Give me ears to hear, mind to understand
The true way to Thy promised land.
Help me, Lord, that I may know
The way in which Thou meanest me to go!

2

Family

Grannie

Memory is a wonderful thing
And I remember summer, autumn, winter, spring
In Ithaca where I was born on a cold February morn
And in all my memories I feel so near
To my life with my Grannie so sweet, so dear
For she was all the mother I ever knew
For my own lovely Mother life was done
And she went to God when she was but twenty-one.

Grannie, I still can see your wrinkled Indian- brown face so fair
Your snow white hair as you struggle with each day's care
For you had a pair of little girls, not yet two
But they got the best of love from you
For they belonged to your only child, now gone.
Mama, please take care of my babies
Were her last words to you.

Grannie, I see you tending with loving care
The flowers that grew on the place every where
Lily of the valley, roses red, yellow, white
Tiger lilies, a riot of color bright.

I see you working in your garden in the early morn
Among lettuce, radishes, beans, corn.
I smell the apple dumplings and the ginger pears
And the jellies, preserves, conserves simmering everywhere
Canned vegetables, yellow, orange, green
One of the prettiest sights I've ever seen.

I remember the warm bonnets you made for me
To keep my head and ears warm when it was below zero in
degree
I hear your voice reading a story each nite
And the prayers we said in the waning light.

I remember the salt bag you kept warm on the stove all day
It was the hot water bottle of that long ago time
I can feel the clothes frozen stiff on the line
And lamp chimneys we used to share
The wet newspapers we used to put down
To catch dirt when we swept the carpet –
And my little Peter Rabbit flannel night gown.

I remember how I used to get up to read at break of day
And how you'd scold me 'cause I'd catch a cold that way
And when my first grade teacher brought me home
To show you how well I read
You smiled graciously. Thank you, you said
And when she'd gone, you looked at me
And said, don't you dare tell her you could read since you were three.

I see your nimble fingers that could tat, knit, embroider, crochet
And the beautiful clothes you made sewing for the wealthy by the day
The rag rugs you made of this 'n' that
The Sunday callers who came to sit on the porch to chat.

And then we moved to Washington, DC with our Dad
How we missed you – the only mother we'd ever had
And when we came back each summer how happy we were
My sister Mary, you, the old house, and me.

Two Grandmothers

Two Grandmothers had I
One from the South, the other from the North
My grandmothers were dears those two
And although each other they scarcely knew
They had two little girls, my sister and me
Left motherless while babies still
But Grannie valiantly took on her daughter's children
And later Grandma patiently helped her son rear his girls ....

But first, it was Grannie
Now Grannie was of average height, slim, and wiry
With a crown of snow white hair
Above a face the color of an Indian and beautiful dark eyes.

People used to ask her if she was
an East Indian and she would laugh
Indeed one story of our roots tells of East Indian blood.

When I was a little girl, she had two brothers and two sisters
still living.
Aunt Evie and Uncle George looked just like Grannie in feature
and coloring
So did Aunt Frank (Frances) and Uncle Charlie, but they were
Caucasian in color like their father.

Grannie was loving, feisty, and hard working. She tended her garden and wasted not a whit of what it gave forth. We ate of its bounty all summer and crisp beautiful fresh vegetables and the good juicy fruit—apples, pears, peaches, cherries, plums, red grapes, purple grapes, blue grapes, red raspberries, black raspberries—that grew on the vines, bushes, and trees in our big sprawling yard. And in the winter from the pantry spilled out these same goodies that Grannie had canned—corn, beans, beets, cabbage—also conserves, preserves, jellies, jams, and plain fruit.

And what I remember most about all this is the good smells.

Grandma Ogle

My Grandma Ogle lived near the University
My sister Mary would often come from classes to see
Her, and being popular always brought along a fellow or two
And Grandma would make them eat – no wouldn't do
Soon boys without Mary would drop by
Grandma would give them lunch, or supper, milk, pie.

Now the time was the beginning of the Great Depression
Much, much worse than this 1982 recession
Parents were poor – there was hardly a student loan
Financially the kids were mostly on their own.

Now Grandma's husband had died when her children were small
So except for what the family gave her, she had nothing at all
But she counted her pennies – hoarded her store
Fed and mothered boys who came to her door.

For years Grandma kept her feeding station in her house by the
side of the road
I know she lightened many a college boy's load.
Now if in heaven one enjoys a good meal
I'm sure Grandma's dispensing manna with zeal.

For all she needs is a spoon and a pot
And she'll make a little into a lot.
For her teacher was Jesus of the fish and the loaves
Of Him Grandma learned how far God's provision goes!

Childhood Memories

An Unusual Day

Mrs. Byrd called Grannie one day
to ask if Annie could come to play
And Grannie said ok.
Then Mrs. Byrd asked Grannie if my sister Mary could meet
Annie at the car stop at Plain and State Street
Now Mary wasn't feeling well that day
So Grannie delegated me and sent me on my way.
I skipped gaily along – it wasn't very far
And soon Annie hopped off the street car.
I said hello to Annie, told her Mary was under the weather
Then held out my hand so we could walk home together.

But Annie said, "No, let's go by Barbara Morrell's a minute"
I didn't want to – and if it was a mess, I was in it
'Cause I was too timid to say, "I can't do that, No!"
I knew nothing else but go
So we went and when we came out
She wouldn't turn when I told her to
And was determined to have her way the whole day through.

So we walked and walked, and I was scared to death
Still we walked and walked some more until I was really out of breath
Finally we came to Six Mile Creek
And I knew I was near Plain Street.
Annie wanted to climb down the bank to play
Suddenly it dawned on me Annie is running away
Else why would she find excuses to keep on walking
And pay no attention to my feeble squawking?

With this discovery I tried to gather my six year old wit
I did and said, "Annie, please wait for me a little bit

I'm hungry and I'm going home to get us some food."
Now Annie must have been in a pretty good mood
She was a few years older than me
And bossed me around as you can see!
And with nothing I said or did would she agree
But miracle of miracles, she said,
"OK, I'll wait for you but hurry, I'm hungry, too."

I was so happy I almost flew up the street.
As I neared home, whom did I meet
But my sister Mary face aflame
Running, running, and calling my name
"Irene, Irene. Here she is Grannie
I found her! I found her!"
And then there was quite a stir
As folks in the neighborhood gathered round
Asking "Irene, where have you been? We've looked all over town."

Now they didn't find Annie 'til long after light of day
And she told everyone I made her run away
Her mother believed her and gave me the blame.
I cried, and my heart was full of shame
That I couldn't make Annie come with me
To my house where she was supposed to be
But dear Grannie believed me and understood
That I'd done the best a six year old could
Thank you, dear Grannie, for all your love and care
Heaven is a beckoning place because you are there!

As for Annie, she ran away all her young life long
Her mother couldn't teach her right from wrong
And in wrongdoing there were always tales of Annie's part
And I'm sure she broke her mother's heart.

Grandma's Pitcher of Blue

From my grandmother came this pitcher of blue
Milk white, soft green, and gold
And in its every beautiful hue
I find the virtue her heart did hold.

Like the white – pure ever her soul
As with grace she played her role
Of being God's child day by day by day
Always she followed and trusted Him along the way.

Always for her the grass was ever green
Such faith and trust is seldom seen
She buried her husband and children five
But thru it all her faith stayed green – alive.

True blue was she to one and all
To her children, grandchildren, friends all
The college boys she used to feed
For during the depression they were really in need.

Yea, the pitcher her virtue does hold
For Grandma was ever often pure white
True blue, and real gold.

A Lovely Mother

A lovely mother stepped outside
To talk with God a little while
He spoke, "In the city fair abide
And give the rapture of your smile.

Still shines forth my promise true
I, the Lord, speak so to thee
I have prepared a place for you
That where I am also you may be.

Here stretch out your helping hand
Here your kindly deeds renew
Here is my own heavenly land
Are many mansions for such as you."

So lovely mother went to sleep
Safe forever in Jesus' sheltering, loving arms
Be still, sad hearts. Do not weep
For you have loved and known her charms.

Yes, a lovely mother has gone to sleep
Softly sweetly, she has gone
Heavenly Father, we pray thee keep
Her until we, too, meet Thy glorious dawn.

What is a Mother Like?

1. Like Lane Furniture, she gets something beautiful going
2. Like Pepsi Cola, she gives her very best
3. Like Better Homes and Gardens Booklets, she solves the most common problems
4. Like Rubber Maid, she provides the little things that help in a big way
5. Like Kodak, she has built in flash
6. Like Kraft American singles, she is the go between
7. Like Fisher toys, you can trust her with a baby
8. Like Quaker State Motor Oil, she's made to help
9. Like Prudential Life Insurance, she is a piece of the rock
10. Like Buliva Watch, Mother is a name you can trust
11. Like Revere Ware, her beauty and performance are everlasting!

Little Girl

Little girl of the 1880's
With your sweet solemn little face
Your pretty hairdo
Your dainty pink dress
And your high-topped black leather shoes
You are beautiful
And I love you
For you grew up to be my mother!

My Mother's Plates

Gold-edged, white and blue
They are all I have
From a mother I never knew.

For you died when I was less than a year
And you only twenty-one
But I hold you ever dear!

I always like to think, dear Mother,
That if you had lived
How we would cherish one another!

Like the birds up on the bough
We would be sitting close
Sharing memories now.

Eating from your plates of blue
And drinking tea
Joy and love to share—just we two.

It was not to be
You are not here
As I sail Life's sea!

But ever since I've been grown
Wherever I have lived
Your plates a shrine I enthrone.

They tell me you were beautiful, fair,
Gentle, loving, kind
In the plates you touched, I hold you ever there
Suspended in time!

Recollections of My Father, Robert H. Ogle

June, 1999

My father was tall, good looking – always impeccably dressed
And as a father to two motherless girls, he was the very best.
Perhaps a little too strict, but now I can see
That he wanted us to be the very best that we could be.

My father grew up in Georgetown and graduated from Old
M Street High
And I guess his ambitions reached the sky.
For he wanted to go to college, but didn't see how
His mother was a widow with two other children
There was no way for her to help him now.

But Bob was determined, so in summer he worked on the
railroad
Saving as much as he could to ease the financial load.
In winter he waited table at the Ithaca Hotel
And thus here he was at prestigious Cornell
But he couldn't stay in a dormitory then
Nor join a fraternity with white college men.

But my father had six colored friends who didn't sit and
moan
All seven of them had rooms in the town they could call
home
So they decided to meet and study together
This they did even in Ithaca's severe winter weather.
Later they decided also to meet and have fun
This made life better for everyone.

And now guess what—they decided to start a fraternity
This they did but it seemed to take an eternity!

Thus was born Alpha Phi Alpha—the first black fraternal
organization in the USA
And now more than ninety years later, it is considered the
foremost black fraternity today.
I don't know how many thousand men strong
But I do know they are some of the finest black men that ever
came along
Scholars, scientists, businessmen, professors, artists, teachers,
Priests, ministers, doctors, lawyers, dentists, preachers.

Alpha Phi Alpha's colors suggested by my father are black and
gold
Denoting black men aiming for the highest and best that life
can hold.

My Sister

Beloved Mary, gone from here
To paths of glory on the other side
Where Life's mystery is made clear
And God Himself does abide.

Here we knew and loved you thru the years
Thru long illness, gallant, brave
But now thru our vale of tears
We must give you back to Him who gave.

So in the communion of saints we believe
And know that God's family all are one
We must try not to grieve
For we hope to see you when day is done.

Until then as God holds us all in His loving heart
And as we keep our memories dear
Dear Mary we are never apart
You safe in Love there, we safe here!

The Passing of Anna

There was a quiet one
Who walked a quiet way
Humbly serving God and us
Steadfastly day by day.

She did not ask but only gave
Of service and love full measure
It seemed then that forever
She would be ours to treasure.

But she stole away from us
Without a word of warning
Back to her God she went
One quiet April morning.

We cannot help but miss her
We cannot help the tears that fall
For so sudden was the taking
That we are stunned by it all.

Because we trust in Thee, O Lord
We will not rant nor rave
But release our sweet Anna
To Thee, the One who gave.

We thank Thee for the loan of her
For these all short, sweet years
And know that faith in Thee
Will wash away all tears.

For My Granddaughter (Angela)
(on her twenty-first birthday)

Angela – Happy Birthday

Behold the sun has risen and set
On seven thousand, six hundred and seventy days
And you are twenty-one!

Within these days you have experienced many things.
Love and laughter
Pain and sorrow
Disappointment and fulfillment
Challenge and accomplishment
Success and failure
Giving and receiving
Anger and forgiveness
Questions and answers.

Now we say you are grown –
But you have been living and learning and growing all your life long.
So hail, Angela, beloved first grandchild
Born on your great grandfather Ogle's birthday
How proud he would have been of you
As I am proud
Proud of your commitments
Proud of each accomplishment
Proud of your triumph over illness.

And my wish is that
You will keep climbing, keep growing
And above all – keep loving
For love is our gift from God
All embracing – all encompassing
Ever flowing back to the giver.

Love,
Grandma

Stephanie

another birthday, another year

Eleven years old and still a dear
Busy – but not skipping down the toy way
But still busy, busy, the livelong day
5th grade student, Girl Scout, Girl Patrol
Now on Saturday giving Computer Science a whirl
Piano lessons, group singing, cooking, dramatics, too
You swim like a fish, yes, busy the whole day through.

You are quite a little actress and starred in the Christmas play
Dependable, competent, and towing the line
But you find time for fun along the way
You ride a bicycle or skate with Mommy or a friend
Lunch with Grammommy, Mrs. B. or Mrs. M
Dolls, paper dolls, puzzles, and games
And by yourself you travel on planes.

But always, you're lovable true blue
And Grandmommy loves you
So Happy Birthday to God's gift to me
My adorable little Granddaughter, Stephanie Marie.

To My Granddaughter

On Your Graduation From High School

Dear Stephanie,

And so you have graduated from High School, favorite girl of mine.

I remember you as a baby – smiling always and always friendly; as a little girl, bright-eyed, adorable. I remember the piano playing, the plays, how you liked to sing, the basketball games. I remember how you and I used to play together – your favorite being "store," and later, games with Mrs. Bass.

Now, a young lady, beautiful in mind and spirit, you go forth to find and prepare for your niche in life. And God has blessed me in you and that I could see this day of your joy and fulfillment.

Grandmommy wishes for you in full measure Love, Love of God, yourself, and your fellow man. When you were a little girl, I said to you, "I love you," and you replied, "I love you, too, Grandmommy. I love everybody." Stephanie, I've never forgotten that, and it has made me a better person.

You have made my life brighter, happier, and when I am gone from you, I want you to always remember how much I love you and that love is a circle that will hold us together wherever we are – for all is life – the finite life here and the infinite that is eternal. I am telling you this so if I go before you, you will know that I am with you always and in God's love, we are never apart.

Here's wishing you Health, Happiness, Peace, and Love, and I look forward to our times together.

Love,

Grandmommy

Christina

Christina – a blessed gift are you
To gladden our hearts – a dream come true
I find you a sweet, sweet relief
From eight years of sorrow and grief.

For you are a part of Philip, my son
And a joy, a joy to everyone
Your Mama keeps you lookin' so perky and neat
You're the best dressed little "gal" on the street
Got the nerve to wear a tiny bracelet on each arm
And show a half smile full of charm.

You're a good little baby, too
You only cry when Mama dresses you
Then, oh how you kick up a fuss
"I don't like this" is what you're telling us
Soon a tooth the fairy will bring
Although you're so young , you can't hold a teething ring.

Great, great granddaughter, you are a pleasure
And all the things you do I treasure
For you this is my prayer
May God keep you ever in his care
And may Mary, our Mother, be with you everywhere.

My Granddaughter

Busy, busy all the day
Skipping down the toy way
From wag-tail doggie and cuddly bear
To naked brown doll minus hair
Building blocks, knocking them down
Riding a tricycle in apartment town
Pushing a button, putting puzzles in place
Into the water, washing the dollie's face
Throwing out the toys, climbing in the box
Scrambling out to take off shoes and sox
Oh, how we love you, adorable one
As we watch you having such good fun.

A Baby
(My Grandson)

A baby is a wonderful thing
A joy for all who pass by
A bundle of love to which we cling
An adorable monarch with demanding cry
A smile or a tear to melt the heart
A rainbow of delight to watch unfold
A miracle from the very start
God's gift fashioned in Love's mold!

The Loss of Philip

On December 21, 1988, three days after his 48th birthday, Philip, my first born and only son dropped dead. The church, my family, and friends rallied round me, perfect examples of acting on the Word.

THE WORD – HONOR THY FATHER AND THY MOTHER. Came my daughter, Melanie, with her family to break the tragic news. She and all my family have daily shown their love and concern.

THE WORD – A FAITHFUL FRIEND IS A STURDY SHELTER. With Melanie came Mary Garnes who stayed with me through the ordeal. Later, lunch in hand for all came Regina Jervay. She stayed with me as did Connie, Mabel, Annie, and many others.

THE WORD – FEED MY SHEEP. Came Father O'Sullivan with communion and prayer. Came Father Bell rushing to catch a plane but taking time for a prayer at the wake. On Christmas Eve, the day of the funeral, Father Kemp put his arms around me, saying, "You can make it, Helen, you have the faith." The faith humbly welcomed and rooted in the Word carried me through – through the fear of being 80 with numerous ailments – How could I make it without Philip. – Fear – Fear – Fear.

THE WORD - I CREATED YOU BECAUSE I LOVE YOU, AND I WILL DO ALL THINGS FOR YOU – THEREFORE DO NOT BE AFRAID. ALL THINGS FOR YOU, THEREFORE DO NOT BE AFRAID. Lord, how can I become more self-sufficient so as not to overburden my daughter?

The Word – I will lift up mine eyes unto the hills from whence cometh my help – My help cometh from the Lord. ***Dear Jesus – How can I bear this grief?***

The Word – Come unto me all you that travail and are heavy laden and I will refresh you. So in the lonely days and sleepless nights humble welcoming these and other Words rooted in me, I was able to act on them and to remember Philip in peace and love!

To My Beloved Son

Good bye, Philip

When you were born on Wednesday, December 18, 1940, at 11 a.m., my heart overflowed with joy. Shortly thereafter I wrote a poem I called First Born.

First Born

This then is the pain of creation
This cleavage within my being
First the joy – the elation
Now the struggle for the freeing
A cry, lusty, strong, unsought - ringing free
Echo of our love song
A man child from you and me.

In writing those words, I never knew how true the line – a cry, lusty, strong. When we brought you home from the hospital you weighed only five pounds, a tiny little bundle of love, but how you could yell. (Oh, how you could yell!) You slept from 6 p.m. to 10 p.m., and in between you yelled. In those days, they were bringing up babies strictly by the book, and you did nothing, absolutely nothing, the book said. You had severe asthma, and many a night I sat up all night with you. But somehow, you grew and prospered.

Good bye, my son

You were a darling little boy
Full of mischief, full of joy
Soft spoken, quiet, short of shy
A pleasure to watch as time went by

I'll garner up the memories. - You liked to listen to good music, and even as a babe would stand up in your crib to listen. You were full of mischievous little tricks, but you always got "A" in Behavior. You had a sense of humor. We'll never forget how one day when you were about three—all of a sudden, you disappeared. The doors were locked, but we couldn't find you. After about half an hour, I said, "I'd better call the police." Grandma Atkins, who had come from across the street to help, said, "Wait, let me look one more time." And there you were—sitting under the table dying of laughter! I should have spanked you, but I was too glad to see you.

Good bye, my son

The memories linger on — I'll remember how you bounced along on those two slue feet—one going east—one going west. Your joy at having a little sister. The city-wide Dental Poster Contest you won. Captain of the Boy Patrol. How delighted you were to get the braces off your teeth. The Lionel trains and the villages, bridges, roads you built for them to travel through. How you liked good music, and how you became a progressive jazz enthusiast. Mary Garnes nicknamed you "Jazz." You liked that name, "Jazz." Your young marriage and fatherhood. How you loved all children, but especially your own.

Good bye, my son

When you were graduated from Birney {Elementary School}, as the principal handed you your certificate, she said, "Old man Philip. You can always depend on him – and get advice from him."

Yes, Philip, you would always tell the truth. "Philip, did you do thus and so? "Yes, Mama." "Why?" "I dunno."

Good bye, Philip

Words you spoke were always true
And we could always depend upon you.
You played the piano with a soft, gentle touch
But because of asthma, with sports couldn't do much
You went to St. John's and played in the band
Rushing off to school, trombone in hand
You went to college, but did not stay
Your fine mind seeking another way
You said you never really wanted to go
But thought we'd be hurt and wouldn't say so.

Good bye, dear son

All my life I remember your gentle, kindly helpfulness to me with never a note of irritation at any request. "But sure, Mama, no problem, no problem!"

I remember when I left home, how you came to me and said so gently, "I packed a box of your poetry books for you, Mama." Thank you, Philip, I'd never had them if it hadn't been for you.

I remember one time I was having (my prayer group) Anawin to Christmas lunch, and everything went wrong. The doorbell rang, and there stood Philip. "I got off early, Mama, so I could help you." And my son, who was a gourmet cook, went to work.

Good bye, my son

Life was difficult and struck you many a blow.
But you have been valiant. This I want you to know
For if you went down to the count of nine
Up you rose time after time
You never made an excuse nor placed any blame
But steadfastly kept on playing the game

So I'm proud of you, my only son
And I say to you – Well done!
For life is not measured by wealth nor note
But whether you kept on rowing your leaky old boat
Philip, now you've anchored it safely to shore
Our Father will give you peace for ever more.

So a final good bye, my son

I'll miss your strong support—how every time you came to my house you did something to help me; how when you went to market you put away everything, packaged the meat into single portions so the freezer and ice box looked like a picture. I'll remember the thoughtfulness of gifts you gave.

So Philip as I stood by you for the last time, I said, "Lord, please help me to kneel," and He did. I put my hands on Philip, and I said, "Lord, I thank you for the love of Philip for 48 years. Philip, you have always been a loving, gentle, kind, and helpful son to me. May your soul rest in peace, and Philip, I will carry you forever in my heart."

Amen. Alleluia

Some Help From Philip

Yesterday was one of those days
When I tried God in many ways
I had to go to the doctor, the taxi was late
And when I got there I had to wait
My fault 'cause I wasn't there on time
And that's the beginning of this corny rhyme.
When I came out of the doctor's I didn't have any change
So I had to find a bank somewhere in range.

On to the police station to get the permit
The cop asked for identification to see if I was legit
Searched through my bag, couldn't find a thing
Friends with purses, does that have a familiar ring?
Finally with the old ID, I was straight
Then couldn't read the figures from Mary Hughes license plate
So the officer, thinkin' I guess, this old lady's a fool
Said he'd call Mary and although he played it cool
He couldn't find her number so I grabbed the book
So we got it together but what a time it took.

Permits safely in my hand I went outside
To look for a cab, home to ride
But the wind took my pretty scarf and it blew
Straight into the filthy muddy gutter – whew
Now I'd already lost my black kid gloves that a.m.
So I said, "Let me get home before I go crazy this p.m."
And just as I stepped out of the taxi door
Here comes Jake to work on the house some more
Then comes my friend to bring the rolls and cake
And down she sat a little visit to make.
Then my sister-in-law strolled over to have a chat
But she did do an errand for me and that was that.

But the hour's getting late, and I look at the setting sun
And sign, "how'll I ever get my day's work done."

When at the door, I heard a key
And here's Philip, my son, lookin' at me
"I got off early, Mama, so I could help you."
And I said, "Thank you, son, and God bless you."
So Philip fetched and carried and helped me cook
He set the table, too, and if you look
The madeira cloth is wrong side out
But now that you know what it's all about
You'll know why I decided to let it be
And that's enough of my tale of misery!
For every dark night brings the sun's gold ray
And mine is having you in my home today.

My Daughter

Daughter, you were a glad surprise
Sweet Melanie with the fine dark eyes
You looked like your Great Grandma Ogle then
But something in you reminds me of my sister time and
time again
Some still say you look like me
But that I could never see.

One thing certain you are yourself – that is true
Product of your heritage but uniquely you
Always self-sufficient sure of your way
You accepted responsibility day by day
For your actions – whether good or bad
And gave to every task the very best you had
Always you knew what you wanted to do
And had the stamina to carry it through!

You really don't like advice, questions, intrusion
In your own way you want to carry things to conclusion
You are neat, capable, a perfectionist
Optimistic – in no way a pessimist
Your heart is kind – loving, too
A beautiful daughter all the way through.

Once in high school you dedicated
A little book of poetry to me
On the fly page you wrote – to my
Mother who taught me to love poetry
So now, dear Melanie, I give to you
Poems and prayers I've written the long years through
And when you are old and gray
I hope you pass them to Stephanie some day
For my mother loved poetry, too
So it's part of us – let us carry it through!

Eighteen Today

Eighteen today! What a thrill for you
May your every wish come true
On this day as your glad heart sings
I give to you my apron strings.

It seems to me but yesterday
The Monday you came our way
Plump, dark-eyed, hair a' curl
Sweet Melanie, a darling baby girl!

Today I still can see your solemn little face
As you crept, talked, walked, and danced a pace
Each little piano tune I still can hear
As they grew more difficult year by year.

First Communion, that, too, I remember
And the doll family growing bigger each December
Graduations and the prizes you've won
For citizenship, scholarship, activities well done.

Little talks we've had through the years
Sunny smiles and childhood's tears
Always I'll remember these things
Still I give to you my apron strings!

If sometimes they were pulled a little tight
It was because I wished to guide you right
But now the bird must try its wings
So I give to you my apron strings!

May our love still grow more dear
As we grow older year by year
And always time without end
Count me, dear daughter, as your friend.

Time Together

A beautiful daughter –
a loving and faithful Mother

A Mother's Day Poem

In the *time that has gone by*
We made a melody – you and I
And on our heartstrings is played
A medley of all the tunes we made
Of love and laughter, joy and tears
Of all the things that happened all the years.

Now that you are grown
And our time is more nearly our own
Still we Mother's listen in memory sweet or sad
To all the songs of days we've had
Holding close what is to be
Precious for all eternity.

In the *time that is Now*
As I behold upon your brow
The splendid beauty of womanhood
I look at my daughter and find her good
Proud am I to have been a part
Of giving you life – and some small start
Along your chosen way
And so on this Happy Day
I thank you for what you are
Your Mother's own Bright Star!

In the *time that is to be*
As we sail Life's challenging sea
I ask your love day by day
Forgiveness where I've failed along the way
A chance to show my love for you
A willingness to pledge anew

My recognition of your right to be
A woman serene in your own destiny
My knowledge that I hold no apron string
And you have every right to do your own thing!

Thus I am bold to speak and say
Thank you for what you are today
And as a proud and loving mother
For a daughter I would have no other.
I pray that God will always bless
My dear daughter with His love, peace, and happiness.

Marea

(My stepmother)

Soft as a fragrant rose
Refreshing as a gentle breeze that blows
Modest like the tiny violet blue
In action – an arrow straight and true
Sturdy – steadfast like the oak tree
Generous in mind and spirit like the rolling sea
Ever there like ivy on the storied wall
Sharing her bountiful gift with all
Thank God for the joy of Marea along the way
Thank God for the love she showered every day.

Marion

Miss Marion was my mother-in-law, I loved her dear
I still see her at her door calling to the children, "Come here."
Then she talked of this or that in her cheery way
Asking them about home or school that day
But always before she said Good bye
"See you at Sunday School" would be her cry
Or "Missed you last week," maybe she'd add
"Come next Sunday, and make me glad."
"Find me now, cause I've got something special for you to do
Cause I know I can always depend on you."
I can hear the children saying still
"I'll be there, Miss Marion," as they smiled at her good will!

I think I see gentle Jesus smiling too
At dear Miss Marion who carried through
His injunction to love the children and the poor
And did it faithfully from her own front door!

3
Of This and That

Glad That I Live Am I

Glad that I live am I
That the sky is blue
Glad for the summer rain
And the fall of dew.

After the sun, the rain
After the rain, the sun.
This is the Way of Life
'Til the work is done.

Grow Nearer the Sky

The world stands out on either side
No wider than the heart is wide
Above the world is stretched the sky
No higher than the soul is high.

The soul can split the sky in two
And let the face of God shine through.
All that we need to do be we low or high
Is to see that we grow nearer the sky!

Heritage

As we walk our country's byways
In summer sun, autumn haze
Our proud heritage we see
Our own America, land of the free!

O blessing more precious than life
O heritage that whether joy or strife
We are free from want, free from fear
Free to pray, to speak loud and clear!

Young America, let's work, play, live
The best of ourselves let's give
Each day that all the world may see
The privilege of living in a Democracy!

What is Beautiful

What is beautiful?
A rose some say
And break of day.

What is beautiful?
A bird in flight
The far-flung night.

And beautiful, too
Like morning dew
The heart and face of you!

You Are Beautiful

You are beautiful
Like days of winter
Buffeted with storms
Sparkling like snow
Seeking warmth and peace!

You are beautiful
Like budding spring
Bright with promise
Reaching forth
Bearing gifts!

You are beautiful
Like summer in full bloom
Flashing beauty
Holding warmth
Offering love!

You are beautiful
Like autumn in flame
Splashing color
Exemplifying God's love
Exuding joy!

You are beautiful
Because you are God's child
Created in His image
Nurtured by His Word
Caressed in His love!

Aye, you are Beautiful!

Serenity

I sit alone in this place
Amid the beauty of earth
The splendor of sky
And all is peace!

I do not hear
The beat of the tom-toms
The sound of dancing feet
I hear only silence.

I do not see
Women at the cooking pot
The children playing
I see only the beauty of nature!

But I can feel
The warm wind at my back
The gentle mist that is rising
The silence enveloping me.

So I sit alone waiting
And the Great Spirit enters
I am open to His Word
I am ready to receive.

And the Great Spirit speaks within me
Receive, my child, the gift of Serenity
You yourself have found it
Just by being still!

For serenity is quiet
It is peace
It is faith, hope and love
It is acceptance of me!

So come apart as you have today
And in the serenity of your heart
Find me. Hear me.
And go forth refreshed!

So take this gift, my child,
To the marketplace
Wherever duty or your heart leads
And walk in peace with your brother!

Years

Years are lovely fragile things
Treasures I'm glad I own
Fruits growing near the springs
From seeds that I have sown.

They lie behind me sharp and clear
The years that I have spent
Their messages concrete and dear
Help me today to live content.

They stretch before an endless road
To which I cannot see the bend
By which the Master lifts a load
Helping me to meet the end.

The year I'm living in today
I hope will be the best of all
To make the past a more pleasant way
The future a vision to enthrall.

Years are lovely fragile things
Treasures that I'm glad I own
Fruits growing near the springs
From seeds that I have sown.

Harbingers

The door I shut at night
Against the winter's cold
The blinds I draw, the lamp I light
I'm safe, content within the fold.

Morning finds work for me
A busy bundle of little things
I light the fire, lift the blind to see
Then lo, my glad heart sings.

Far out beyond the kitchen door
Births a tender, new, growing thing;
Eats a robin, then grubs for more
O, happy harbingers of spring!

My hands drop idle, my eyes overflow
At sight of birthing flower, hungry bird.
There comes a warmth, an inner glow
As the soul feels the prayer it cannot word.

O dainty flower, newly born
Hungry bird chirping notes of cheer
What a message for the morn
Winter has gone, spring is here!

Mountain Thoughts

The land like a checkerboard lies
In hues of brown and green
Under the cloud caught skies
Nature's grandeur rests supreme.

The mountains tower over all
Rising majestic to the sky
Hugging close thick and tall
Trees, moved only by the wind's changeling cry.

Here once no foot ever trod
Nor whirling wheel ever turned
But in majesty known only to God
The earth lived and learned.

Lord, now may the heart rest still
And garner for itself Thy glory
Nurturing in mind and will
The wonder of creation's story.

And in the rod, the road, the wheel
That now dot this once barren land
May man in his dominion feel
The omnipotence of God's almighty hand.

Beauty

I like the beauty that Nature holds
Upon her ample breast
Green grass, wet black earth
Ocean wide, tiny violet there may rest.

I like the things that Nature grasps
Within her outstretched hand
Soft breeze, glittering snow, falling rain
To succor all her bounteous land.

I like the crown that Nature wears
Upon her wind-swept hair
Fleecy cloud, winging bird, jeweled sun
All are there.

A Time in History

The recent riots in Los Angeles have brought to the surface many deep and perplexing questions, some old, some new. In addressing these questions, there seems to be one difference from now and yesteryear – a sincere desire on the part of the races to better understand each other and to earnestly try to implement a workable solution.

In addressing this need for understanding, one question that whites and some blacks ask is, "Why are blacks so resentful and angry and why when something goes wrong, do they riot—plunging and pillaging their own neighborhoods as well as other people's property and persons."

Well, let's begin at the beginning. Wait, don't say the past is past. Don't you take pleasure in saying things like, My great grandfather came over on the Mayflower or My mother's grandmother was a pioneer wife in Minnesota, or I am descended from Thomas Jefferson or Robert E Lee or Eli Whitney or My great, great uncle James B. Blank was first to fall in the Battle of Richmond.

Well, the American Negro has none of this history. He was brought here as a slave and many of these slaves were kings or princes or tribal chief or Medicine Man. All this was stripped from him—his ancestry, his family, his language, his pride—even his name.

It was against the law to teach a slave to read or write, although some kind masters did. George Washington Carver's mistress taught him and look what he accomplished. The poor white farmer in the South is much better off because of Carver.

When the Negro was set free, he was unable to read or write or use money, given not a quarter, not an ox or one tool, nor a quarter of an acre. Many were forced to work for shares, and thus was born the infamous share cropping system.

Many kind masters having nothing else to give, gave the emancipated slave a piece of land. Yet much of this land has been wrested away by lies, deceit, and fraud. I have read and seen on the television much material about this, and it is too complicated to go into here. Nor it is not easy to throw off such things when they are passed along from generation to generation, and each generation has tales to add.

Even I and countless others, educated or not educated, were taught pride, responsibility, effort, and hard work by loving family. We were taught to reach for the stars, and it was this upbringing that prompted me to write for my pupils long before the phrase "black pride" became a byword.

Not my color, but what I do
Is what counts the long day through
It's how I think deep down inside
And whether I carry myself with pride
It's how I try a nicer child to be

Yet those of us with pride and an incentive could tell many a tale of discrimination, the turning the back when one asks directions, the riding on the back of the bus, the difficulty in obtaining work for which one is prepared, the difficulty in obtaining promotion, etc.

I could relate a few hundred that involved me or my family or my friends. How can one help but feel resentful. How can one help but feel inferior. One is not in the history books; no black children were pictured in the textbooks nor in the visual aid materials.

The middle class Negro's head is bloody but unbowed. When we could not attend the theaters, we went to New York. We brought the Clare Tree Major plays here for our children. We fostered many outstanding drama groups. We wrote books about blacks and our history. We started our own history. We started our own organizations.

But it is the ghetto person about whom we will discuss. What about him, poor, disadvantaged, without education or job training. In short, without hope. What about him.

Not My Color

I will live today better than before
Perfecting little things more and more
Thinking not of creed or color of face
But how to serve the whole human race!

Not my color but what I do
Is what counts the long day through
It's what I think deep down inside
And whether I carry myself with pride.

It's what I owe my neighbor (the world), not what he (the world) owes me
It's how I try a nicer child to be
It's how I help make the world a better place to live
Now how much I get, but how much I give.

And as I work at school each day
Doing the very best I can
I know my world neighbors work and play
Just like every little American.

Moon Talk

(written in 1929 before Man walked on the moon)

O moon, way up in the sky
So round, so big, so bright
I talked to you as you sailed high
One lovely summer night.

I told you Life had hurt me
You laughed saying it had hurt others, too
Was that because you were not in sympathy
Or do mortals demand too much from you?

New Horizons

We look around us in despair
At the chaos man has wrought
Daily we struggle from care to care
Where will it end our thought?

"Dear Lord, may tomorrow better be!"
Humbly we pray when day is done
Then hope springs anew when we see
At dawn, the glorious sun.

Now our faith is strong, our purpose clear
For in each golden dawn we know
A new horizon does appear
Blazing the way for us to go.

New horizons! What precious thought
In answer to our humble prayer
In them we may teach and be taught
To serve all peoples everywhere.

This must a teacher give
To those who come her way
A chance to fully, richly live
In peace and brotherhood from day to day.

God's Bouquet

To little flowers peeping from the grass
I will nod a cheery hello as I pass
Brown-eyed Susan, rose, a dainty pink
Yellow daffodil, fair lily at the water's brink.

God made children like the flowers
To be happy in sun and showers
Each one He made differently
None just like you or just like me.

To little children playing in the grass
I will nod a cheery hello as I pass
Brown-eyed Susan, Rose a dainty pink
Yellow Daphne, fair Lilly at the water's brink.

For all belong to God's bouquet
And are my neighbors along life's way.

Love, Lost, and Found

At last I've found Love
He came tripping down my way
I threw myself within his arms
And laughed the livelong day!

Now I've lost Love
He skipped gaily from my door
Leaving me broken hearted
But richer than of yore!

The Person Sitting Next to Me

The person sitting next to me
Christ tells me is my brother.
For we must first love God
And then one another.

So the person sitting next to me
I now look at with love
For she is a gift, a mandate from God above.

So I look at her with new eyes
And perhaps with a bit of surprise
For I find she's a lot like me!

She, too, has likes and dislikes – to that I must agree
She, too, has hopes and fears
Her life has laughter and tears.

And sometimes feel blue
She has lost folks who are dear
Or may be alone or lonely here.

So God, take my hand in your hand
Lead me so that I may understand
That the person sitting next to me
Needs my love – for she is part of Thee!

Slender Days

Now come the slender days
When all once woven is worn bare
Stripped of the beloved's ways
Which anchored it safely there.

Now must you gather up the threads
And weave a pattern plainer still
Its design, like well-worn treads
Must be painted bright with master skill.

Make the tears glisten like jewels bold
Let memories brighten the somber hue
And in this simpler pattern bravely hold
Close, what love alone gave to you.

Then shall you know that what is fine
And good, and brave, and gay
Is but a part of God's great design
To lead us, thru love, to a brighter day.

Up from the Meadows

Up from the meadows rich with corn
Clear in the cool September morn
The clustered spires of Frederick stand
Green-walled by the hills of Maryland.

Round about them orchards creep
Apple and peach trees fruited deep
Fair as the garden of the Lord
To the eyes of the famished rebel horde.

On that pleasant morning in early fall
When Lee marched over the garden wall
Over the mountains winding down
Horse and fast, into Frederick town.

Forty flags with their silver stars
Forty flags with their crimson bars
Flapped in the morning wind, the sun
Of noon looked down and saw not one.

Up rose old Barbara Fritchie, then
Bowed with her fourscore years and ten
Bravest of all in Frederick town
She took up the flag the men hauled down.

In her attic window the staff she set
To show that one heart was loyal yet.

Up the street came the rebel tread
Stonewall Jackson riding ahead
Under his slouched hat left and right
He glanced – the old flag met his sight.

"Halt!" - the dust brown ranks stood fast
"Fire" - out blazed the rifle blast
It shivered window pane and sash
It rent the banner with seam and gash.

Quick as it fell from its broken staff
Dame Barbara snatched the broken staff
She leaned far out on the window sill
And shook it forth with a royal will.

"Shoot, if you must, this old gray head
But spare your country's flag," she said.
A wave of sadness, a blush of shame
Over the face of the leader came.

The nobler nature within him stirred
To life at that woman's deed and word
"Who touches a hair of your gray head
Dies like a dog. March on," he said.

All day long thru Frederick Street
Sounded the tread of marching feet
All day long, that free flag tossed
Over the eyes of the rebel host.

Ever its torn folds rose and fell
On the noble winds it loved so well
And thru the hill gaps sunset light
Shone over it with a warm good night.

Barbara Fritchie's work is o'er
And the rebel rides on his raids no more
Honor to her! And let a tear
Fall for her sake on Stonewall's bier.

Over Barbara Fritchie's grave
Flag of freedom and Union wave!

Peace and order and beauty draw
Round thy symbol of light and law
And ever the stars above look down
On thy stars below in Frederick town!

Aralessa

I stood a mountain stream beside
And watched its waters cool and clear
Come tumbling down the mountainside
Birthing a river to meander far from here.

I walked a mountain meadow – lush and green
And marveled at each lovely flower
Pink, red, yellow, aquamarine
Nestling in its snow-capped rocky bower.

As I trudged the mountain road that morn
I touched the redwood and the pine
Mighty trees that eons ago were born
And thought, surely Lord, the world is thine.

Today far from stream or tree
From flowered mountain capped with snow
I have only hallowed memory
And will forever cherish its glow.

Aralessa, friend of long years
When I was asked on behalf of friends, to greet
You whose friendliness endures
And enriches everyone you meet.

I wondered what we could say
Worthy of so fine a friend
Then I thought of that mountain far away
And now I know its glow shall serve its end.

For like the mountain stream, you are sweet and calm
Spending your friendship far and wide
Your serenity, a quiet balm
A dependable softness in life's hectic tide!

In Friendship We Keep

When you part from your friend, you grieve not
For that which you love most in him may be clearer in his
absence
As the mountain to the climber is clearer from the plain.

And let there be no purpose in friendship save the deepening
of the spirit
For love that seeks aught but the disclosure of its own mystery
is not love
But a net cast forth; and only the unprofitable is caught.

And let your best be for your friend
If he must know the all of your tide, let him know its flood also
For what is your friend that you should seek him with hours to
kill?
Seek him always with hours to live.

For it is his to fill your need, but not your emptiness
And in the sweetness let there be laughter, and sharing of
pleasures
For in the dew of little things, the heart finds its morning and
is refreshed.

Life Goes By

A little dreaming by the way
A little toiling day by day
A little pain, a little strife
A little joy – and that is life!

A little short-lived summer's morn
When joy seems all so newly born
When one day's sky is blue above
And one bird sings – and that is love!

A little sickening of the years
The tribute of a few hot tears
Two folded hands, the failing breath
And peace at last – and that is death!

Just dreaming, loving, dying so
The actors in the drama go
A flitting picture on a wall
Love death the themes – but that is all!

The Gift of Faith

Faith is a gift of God. It is not a material that can be seen, heard, tasted, or touched; but is as real as anything that can be perceived with these senses. One can be aware of Faith as easily as one can be aware of earth.

Faith is as certain as the evidence of water. Faith is as sure as the taste of an apple, the fragrance of a rose, the sound of thunder, the sight of the sun, the feel of a loving touch.

Hope is a wish, a longing for something not now possessed, but with the expectation of getting it. Faith adds surety to the expectation of hope. Faith comes by hearing, and hearing by the word of God. Faith takes God at His word whatever He says.

I have faith in Him, not in my faith.
The trial of my faith is more precious than gold.
Freedom rests, and always will, on individual responsibility, individual integrity, individual effort, individual faith.

Faith is the grave of care.
Faith is the awareness of utter helplessness without God.

This body is my house, it is not I.
Triumphant in this faith I love and die.
Faith is the substance of things hoped for, the evidence of things not seen.

No vision and you perish
No ideal and you are lost
Your heart must ever cherish
Some faith at any cost.

Works is faith made perfect.
The test of our faith is our eagerness to proclaim the good news.

He who loses money loses much; he who loses a friend, loses more;
but he who loses faith, loses all.
Faith is the eyesight of the soul.
The just shall live by faith.

A traveler crossed a frozen stream
In trembling fear one day
Later a teamster drove across
And whistled all the way

Great faith and little faith alike
Were granted safe convoy
One had the pangs of needless fear
The other all the joy

It is not the greatness of my faith that moves mountains,
but my faith in the greatness of God.

Quiet Ways

I long for peace
Beside a quiet stream
When days are pleasant
A fireside by which to dream
When wild winds blow.

For I am weary of the strife
The strains of humdrum days
The dog-eat-dog of daily life
Dear Lord, for me the quiet ways!

The book, the ball, the easy chair
The window on the quiet street
The chance my thoughts to share
With the family and friends I meet
Before I die to draw closer, Lord
To enjoy the vision of thy Reward!

A Teacher's Prayer

Look at the children
Really look and what do you see
Warm brown eyes looking straight at me
Eyes that question what will I do, what will I say
How will I treat this child today.

Do I feel his need and try to understand
This gift from God as close to my hand
Will I condemn his faults, put him down
Forget my smile – show only my frown.

Help me, Lord, guide my way
That I may be a worthy teacher today.

Love, Come Softly Into My Heart

Love, come softly into my heart
That I may welcome thee unafraid
Do not frighten me at the start
For I am waiting – new made.

Touch me sweetly with understanding
With gentle fingers that I may trust
Let our hands in confidence clinging
Because thou will and I must.

Caress me with thine eyes
As the bees the flowers adore
Tell me in words only love may devise
That I am the one forevermore.

Then take me in thine arms
And kiss me sweetly in our bliss
Whisper to me of my charms
And I will answer with a kiss.

Speak to me of love, my dear
Of all that you hope for we two
And I will make reply without fear
And whisper of all my love for you.

Year's End

The year is dying in the red
The brown of wind-blown leaves
The shorter days, the longer nights
The naked-stripped immodest trees.

My heart is dying with the year
Breaking with the wind-blown leaves
Hating days, dreading nights
Loathing such thoughts as these.

Come gentle snow and cover us both
The dying year and me!

April Hill

Spring walked in the other day
In her arms a lovely bouquet
New leaves made a garland for her hair
Birds circled in the freshened air
March winds at her back a-blowing
May beckoning? in colors glowing
Serene she stood on April hill
Midst iris, forsythia, and jonquil
She touched sun, rain drop, bird with her outstretched hand
And smiled upon her spring clad land.

Now and Long Ago

Wherever you live, once long ago
An Indian stood with arrow and bow
Wherever our smoking chimneys rise
Indian smoke once rose to the skies.

Giant tractors cut the grain
Where buffaloes wandered o'er the plain
Thousands and thousands of cattle graze
Where Indians hunted in Indian days.

Noisy autos roll down a street
Where once crept moccasined Indian feet
Our trains go rushing on shiny rails
Where once the Indians made their trails.

Where you now sleep in your bed at night
Indians slept in the campfire light
And where you read a book today
Children played in their Indian way.

Wee Children's Poems

God's world is wonderful, beautiful to see
With wind and wave and tall, tall tree.

Autumn, summer, winter, spring,
God made each wonderful living thing.

Twinkling stars that shine at night
Daytime sun so warm, so bright.

Soft rain that goes patter, patter
Happy little squirrels that chatter.

Baby chicks, pigeons that coo
Sweet little flowers of every hue.

Happy children to work and play
Parents caring for us night and day.

Baby in his bed, bird in his nest
God has given each one the house that is best.

Over it all our Father above
Watching over us with His Love.

God made sun and sent the showers
For He cares for all the pretty flowers.

I'm happy when I work and when I play
For Jesus takes care of me every day.

I like to come to Sunday school
We sing and talk about the Golden Rule.

I say my grace before I eat
To thank my God for bread and meat.

Every night my prayers I say
Asking Jesus to watch over me until day.

When I wake up I smile
Then I pray to Jesus a little while.

Essence

A beautiful rose breathes and dies
But the essence ever in the heart lies
The sun goes down but rises with the dawn
Bringing comfort and promise to the forlorn
Rain comes and goes and air is fresher still
Thus it is by God's love and good will
That our dear ones leave their fragrant essence when they go
God tells us this and thus it is so!

Three Little Boys

Three little boys were talking
One lovely summer day
And I leaned out of the window
To hear what they had to say.

The prettiest thing I ever saw
Said the first little lad
Was a pony at the circus
I wanted him awful bad.

The prettiest thing I ever saw
The second little lad said
Was a bird in Grandpa's garden
All black and white and red.

Said the third little lad
With grave and gentle grace
The prettiest thing I ever saw
Was just my teacher's face.

Night Thoughts

The night has a thousand eyes
The day but one
Yet the light of the whole world dies
With the dying sun.

The mind has a thousand eyes
The heart but one
Yet the light of the whole world dies
With the dying sun.

Homes

There are homes of brick and wood
Of stone, snow, mud, and hide
They shelter us from the storm
And keep us safe and warm inside.

There is home also where the heart wants to be
A lover's arms, a mother's breast, a friend's dear hand
Where we can be in weal or woe
And know that someone will understand.

But the house may fall or be torn down
And lover, parent, or friend be no longer there
Or somehow fail to meet our deep need
And we are left with no one to care.

But he who makes his home with God
And lets God dwell in Him, there forever God will stay
And we will be nurtured by a never ending flow
Of love and faith and peace – beacons to guide the way.

Evolution

A fine mist and a planet
A crystal and a cell
A jelly fish and a saurian
And a place where cave men dwell
This a sense of love and duty
A face turned from the clod
Some call it evolution
And others call it God

Evolution, Too

A picket frozen on duty
A mother starved for her brood
Socrates drinking the hemlock
And Jesus on the road
And millions who humble and meander
The straight hard pathway trod
Some call it consecration
Others call it God

Today

Said one, “I am poor today
Nothing to give have I
Nor to lend, nor to share
And so I must pass you by.”

Said another “I am rich today
In each sparkling new hour
Free to serve and to share
This is my God given power.”

Come Read to Me Some Treasured Poems

Come read to me some treasured poems
Some simple and heartfelt lay
That shall soothe this restless feeling
And banish the thoughts of day

Not from the grand old masters
Not from the bards sublime
Whose distant footsteps
Echo o'er the corridors of time

Read from some humbler poet
Whose songs gushed from his heart
As showers from the clouds of summer
Or tears from the eyelids start

Who through long days of labor
And nights devoid of ease
Still heard in his soul the music
Of wonderful melodies

Such songs have power to quiet
The restless pulse of care, and
Come like the benediction
That follows after prayer

Then read from the treasured poems
The poem of thy choice
And lend to the rhyme of the poet
The beauty of thy voice

And the night shall be filled with music
And the cares that infest the day
Shall fold their tents like the Arabs
And as silently steal away.

Depression Song

I saw a house upon a hill
And visioned your quiet presence there
So much it seemed a part of you
Almost I heard your step upon its stair.

If this house were yours and mine dear
What a haven it would be
A still small paradise of love
Heaven for our new-found ecstasy.

But I cannot buy you a house upon a hill
Nor in this wide world anywhere
The only haven I can offer
Are these strong arms for you to share.

Too poor am I to sing of the love
My heart holds dear
I only pray you somehow reach
The lines I've written here.

Friend

There is a place where I may go
And be myself alone
No matter how ill winds may blow
My friend's house is His own.

There the world is bravely bright
Care once again has flown
I plainly see God's holy light
My friend's house is His own.

Wind and Wave

Wind and wave, sky and sea
What is the song they sing to thee
Of valiant men that once roamed this shore?
Of strong voices now stilled for evermore?

Wind and wave, sea and sky
Hearken to my feeble cry
Let me lift my eyes to behold
Azure blue or stars of gold.

Or lower them to try to keep
The secrets of the boundless deep
Wind and wave, sky and sea
Help me understand thy mystery!

Teacher, Look Around You

We look around us in despair
At the chaos man has wrought
Daily we struggle from care to care
Where will it end our thought?

Dear Lord, may tomorrow better be
Humbly we pray when day is done
Then hope springs anew when we see
At dawn the glorious sun.

Now our faith is strong, our purpose clear
For in each golden dawn we know
A new horizon does appear
Blazing the way for us to go.

New horizons! What precious thought
In answer to our humble prayer
In them we may teach and be taught
Service to all peoples everywhere.

Thus must a teacher give
To those who come her way
A chance to fully richly live
In peace and brotherhood from day to day.

I Saw a Great Tree Fallen

I saw a great tree fallen
Upon a busy street
Sprawled its mighty arms
Silent, its great heart beat.

Long had it stood there
In frost and sleet and rain
Much had it seen there
Of love and poignant pain.

Old School

Long ago a tree stood straight and strong
'Til a sturdy woodsman came along.

Some clay thoughtlessly kicked aside
A workman gathered far and wide.

Later as brick and wood
Tree and clay met where no building stood.

From early morning 'til set of sun
Craftsmen worked until the task was done.

Behold a building then did stand
Empty upon the once barren land.

Now the doors were opened wide
And little children rushed inside.

Look at her now, mellow with years
Warmed by smiles, washed with tears.

A little stooped with long responsibility
But full of wisdom and gentility.

A little heavier than when she was born
But proud, yes proud to be shopworn!

And as the aged do
She sits and reminisces, too.

Fondly she remembers the clay
Gathered on a distant day.

To make her walls sturdy and strong
To shelter the children who came along.

Ah, yes, the children, for them she was made
For what greater use could a brick have been laid?

For God did hallow the brick and wood
That made a school where children could

Be molded in the image of Him who came
To be a Teacher – bless His holy name!

Picture

From this window I can see
A tall and lonely cypress tree
A distant house upon a hill
The shadow from a whippoorwill
The shimmering lake beneath the moon
The flush of a dawn that comes too soon
Too soon for with the coming of the day
I must rise and with my thoughts away!

My Heart

I gave my heart to you
To have, to hold for aye
You took it gently and it drew
From your heart the love it gave reply

For years it pulsed with thine
Content, secure, protected there
I was yours and you were mine
What matter whether joy or care

Then you dropped my heart and it fell
In shattered pieces to the dust
You stepped on it uncaring
And left it there to rust

It has waited all the years
For you to stop by again
To wash the dust with tears
And love me now as then!

Love

Love is a holy word
Verdant, vibrant, ever growing
Faith, Hope, with Love the powerful third
From the Blood of the Lamb ever flowing!

Tryst

Now the night comes dwindling down
To hide the garish of the day
And all my thoughts are gathered round
You, my love, so far away

The sky weeps
The earth sleeps
My heart keeps
Tryst with you

Thoughts

Lo, spring is near again
Bud and flower here again
My heart may sing again
Of hope and joy

I like to walk in the rain
And feel it upon my face
For it washes away my pain
And I become a part of space.

4
Holidays

New Year 1998

We have a New Year – 1998
And so we sit and meditate.
Like Janus – the two-faced God who looked both ways
So we think of past and present days
As we look back at 1997 and all the years before
What do we find when we think of those days of yore?

Well, sorrow for loved ones no longer here
As we try to remember them without a tear
We hold them close to our heart
And know that in love we are never apart.
We think of our children and their adorable ways
That brightened those long-ago days.

Maybe you did not have children but you had some child or person to love
And every child, friend, or person is a blessing from above.
We think of working days, of travel time,
Of more things than I can crowd into this rhyme
But those experiences of love, joy, and sorrow
Help prepare us to meet each tomorrow.

So we turn our faces to the New Year 1998
And we ponder what will be our fate
We don't know, do we, but with surety we can state
There'll be mirth, love, and fun
Good times and some bad times for everyone
I look forward to having my 90th birthday
And whatever else happens – all I can say
Is I'm thankful for my time
And with faith, love, and trust in the Lord divine
I'm content 1998 to face
And I hope I can live it with grace.

A Valentine Thank You Note
February 14, 1988

Dear Family and Friends,

Valentine's Day comes once a year
A day of love and good cheer
Dear to me in a special way
'Cause it happens to be my birthday.
But this year it was just great
For it clocked my years at ten times eight!
And the Brown's hosted a Birthday Tea
Making the day extra super for me.
Friends and relatives gathered near
As they have through thick and thin
Every day of the year.

And in each of your faces I could see
Pictures etched in my memory
Of all the happenings good and bad
Of all the love and joy I've had
Of all the support when things went wrong
Bringing to my heart a glow and a song
Of praise to Him who has seen me through
And given me wonderful gifts like you—
For she who has a family—a circle of love
Surely has a great and lasting gift from above
And she who has a friend has a treasure
And no weight of gold or silver is worth that measure
So thank you all for being here with me
At my lovely, lovely Birthday Tea.

Thank you for all the gifts you bore
Gold earrings, toiletries, books galore
Paschal lamb, stationery, lovely gown set
Coat hangers, pearl combs, the silver barrette
For handmade cross-stitch, original water color, too

For fragrant flowers, plants, tapes, merci beaucoup
Thanks for money, gift certificate, hankies—each thing
Your generous, gracious hearts could bring
Mass cards, birthday cards, Valentines, the lunch date
Slippers, champagne—everything was just great
Gracias for the afghan of pink and gray
The butterfly scene, potpourri, and sachet
The blue and white dish for my collection
Pictures, frames—all the gifts were just perfection.
Thanks to those who couldn't make it on that day
But sent a card, a gift, or a loving thought my way.

Thanks to all my friends and kinfolk tried and true
For the best gift in all the world was YOU!!!

Love,
Helen

Valentines

Roses are red
Violets are blue
Sugar is sweet
So are you.

One, two, buckle my shoe
Sweet darlin' I love you.

Pretty girl lookin' so fine
Won't you be my Valentine.

Gee, I love you no end
Please be my Valentine friend.

Lovely lady, you suit me to a "T"
I want you my Valentine to be.

Three, four, shut the door
If you'll be my Valentine, I'll never ask for more.

Green and yellow, pink and blue
For my Valentine, I choose you.

Apple, orange, peach, and pear
You're the best Valentine anywhere.

One and one make two
For my Valentine, I choose you.

Ice cream, candy, sugar, and spice
For my Valentine, you Oh so nice.

Ice cream, candy, cake, and ice cream
Friendly Valentine you're a dream.

Creamy white, lavender, and blue
Please be my Valentine, I love you true.

Up and down about the town
My beautiful Valentine in a pretty gown.

A smile on your lips. A rose in your hair
Please by my Valentine so fair.

Rosemary, basil, sage, and thyme
Lovely Valentine for you I made this rhyme.

Seven, six, five, four, and three
You're just the Valentine for me.

Sunlight, moonlight, star shine
Pretty Valentine, please me mine.

Young in heart you'll always be
That's why you're just the Valentine for me.

Emerald, diamond, ruby, and pearl
Please be my precious Valentine girl.

Bluebird, cardinal, and dove
To my Valentine, I sing of love.

Violin, flute, music in the air
I sing of love to you, Valentine Lady Fair.

Pretty ribbons, laces, too
Dear Valentine, how I love you.

Marjoram, tarragon, parsley, and bay
Please be my Valentine today.

Carrots, radishes, celery, too
Glad my Valentine friend is you.

Cocoa, coffee, tea, lemonade
As Valentine friends, we've got it made.

Hot cocoa, coffee, or tea
You're just the Valentine for me.

Ribbons, lavender, and old lace
See my Valentine's pretty face.

Mirror, mirror on the wall
My Valentine's the best of all.

Look at you so trim and neat
My Valentine, ain't you sweet.

Gee, I'm just droppin' by
For a friendly Valentine, "Hi."

Three, six, nine
Be my Valentine.

Three little kittens come to say
Please be my Valentine today.

Buttons and bows, buttons and bows,
You're my Valentine everyone knows.

Come, let's go skate on the ice
My friendly Valentine, you're so nice.

Chinese puzzle, not ah so
You're my friendly Valentine, you know.

Needles, pins, and sew a fine seam
For a friendly Valentine, you're my dream.

New copper penny, a silver dime
Gee, I love my friendly Valentine.

One, two, and skip to my Lou
Whose my Valentine? Why it's you!

Necklace, earrings, a pretty ring
As my Valentine, you're just the thing.

Summer, winter, spring, or fall
As a Valentine, you're the best of all.

Bluebird, nightingale, dove
To my Valentine, I sing of love.

Red, blue, green, and yellow
As a Valentine, you're a jolly good fellow.

Thanksgiving Day

Now come the thankful days
When we count our blessings one by one
We think of life's pleasant ways
As we pause when day is done!

You say you didn't get that something new
For Mama didn't have enough money to go round
But our Blessings are always all too few
When we keep our eyes close to the ground.

But let's look up in joy and smile
At whatever good has come our way
Let's think of what we have that's worthwhile
And this will gladden all our day.

We have the beauty of the earth
The love of one another
And we have our own self worth
Good health, and each other.

So on this Thanksgiving Day
I am thankful for home and school
For my dear family and each dear friend I pray
That God continue to bless as we follow His Golden Rule.

Thanksgiving Blessings

Let us give thanks for God's great gifts
Of Life, of Love, of Laughter, of Children
Of fun and fellowship, of food, and family
But most of all, for each other
For no man is an island, no man walks alone
Without others he has no support, no touch, no reason for being.

So today I humbly thank God for each of you – (names) –
For all of our relatives
I pray for those not here present
I pray for those who have passed

Heavenly Father,

We offer Thanksgiving for all your goodness and loving kindness and mercy to all men. Let us be ever mindful that all is gift. Help us to give thanksgiving for these gifts not just today, but every day. Fill us with your gifts and make us always eager to serve you in Faith, Hope, and Love.

In Jesus' Name, Amen

Thanksgiving Prayer Verses

Let us pray –

Teach me, Father, when I pray
Not to ask for more
But rather let me give my thanks
For what is at my door
For food and drink, for gentle rain,
For sunny skies above
For home and friends, for peace and joy
But most of all for Love

Heavenly Father

For the beauty of the earth
For the glory of the skies
For the love that from our birth
Over and around us lies
For the wonder of each hour
Of the day and of the night
Hill and vale, and tree and flower
Sun and moon and stars of light
Lord of all, to Thee we raise
This our hymn of grateful praise

Amen

For the circle of the day
For rest when evening falls
For family and friends
For food and flowers and fun

For Thy mercies Lord
For Thy goodness in all that we have
And in the gift of the loving sacrifice of Thy son
For Thy love and His
For the love of Helen and Mary and their friendship, Lord
We give Thee thanks.

Amen

America and Other Nations and Christmas Time

Let us as we wend our homeward way
Think of the world as it is today
Know that the wide world o'er
Christmas cannot be celebrated as of yore
In many nations hearts cannot sing
At the birth of our Saviour King.

Little Dutch shoes sit by an empty chimney place
English carols are sung in unheated space
Whence will come fruit for the Swedish Xmas tree
Food for the hungry of Germany
How will *all* the Santas in *all* the lands
Have gifts for little children's eager hands.

Listen while I give the answer clear
The same today and all the year
America, America, our own democracy
Blessed with peace and plenty from sea to sea
America, America, your land and mine
Remember the birth of the Saviour Divine!

Know that He who was born one holy night
Wants comfort for His children black and white
Within your heart, hear His prayer
"O feed My hungry everywhere
Clothe My naked on every shore
And I will bless you more and more!

My little children – O forget not them
For I was once a child in Bethlehem
Bring now your gifts as gifts were brought to me
A new born Babe in Bethany
America! With the flags of all nations unfurled
Bring My love and Merry Christmas to *one* world!"

An Acrostic for Christmas

C is for Christmas with its bright cheer
For candy and children, a happy time of year
For the cards we send, the carols we sing
For candles that glow, church bells that ring!
Best of all C is for Christ, a gift of love
Peace and redemption sent by Our Father above!

H is hark the herald angels sing
H is hail to the newborn Christ, our King
H is for your health, happiness, too
As we wish a Happy Holiday to all of you!

R is the road Joseph and Mary trod
To Bethlehem for the birth of the Son of God
R is for room - all were full in the town
Nowhere to lay the sweet head of the infant down.

I is for the inn that was full that night
I is for the innkeeper who saw a mother's plight
For the infant who was the Messiah foretold
And for interest in a story, ever new but ages old!

S is for the sky that Holy Night
For the star that shone there clear and bright
For sheep and the shepherds who found their way
To the newborn babe 'sleep on the hay!

T is for the three Wise Men who traveled far
Led to the Holy Infant by the Christmas Star
For the three gifts they offered of myrrh,
frankincense, and gold
As they knelt in homage at love made manifold.

M is the miles traveled to meet a decree
And for the man, Joseph, part of the Holy Mystery
M is for Mary, Mother of the Holy Babe
And for the humble manger wherein He was laid.

A is for the animals in that lowly place
Who, on that first Christmas, behold a Baby's face
A is for the angels who hovered near
And all of us who are gathered here.

S is for this season of joy and mirth
For the silence of the night of the Holy Birth
For the swaddling clothes the baby wore
For the simple prayer, "O Come, Let Us Adore."

His Gift

When Christ was born one holy night
That first Christmas so long ago
A lowly manger was made bright
By a star shining with heaven's glow.

That star was followed from afar
By shepherds and wise men who came to seek
The Babe – Savior of all mankind
Born of Mary, mild and meek.

A manger of straw was His humble bed
A promise of Life His gift so rare.
From the Bethlehem hills His peace still shines
Teaching us to love our brothers everywhere.

Two Thousand Years Ago

Two thousand years ago
A star shone bright
Holy angles sang Joy
Shepherds walked that night

Three kings came bearing gifts
Cattle bent low
Silent night – blessed night
All heaven aglow

Joseph watched in wonder
A mother smiled
And in a manger bed
The Holy Child!

First Angel

The earth is beautiful tonight
All bathed in God's holy light

Know ye not, Holy Christmas is here
For just this hour may we show
Our presence to earth bound mortals below
Now all angel prayers the earth shall bless
All angel wings the earth caress

On this night the world does see
We holy angels from eternity

Our God is one of love, my dear
We must love our brothers here
And there in every far away land
We must try hard to understand
Their different ways of work and play
And not mind to what God they pray

Now is a rare gift offered thee
A wonderful story you are privileged to see
As men saw it long ago and knew its worth
Little Angel, tell them of Christ's birth.

Christmas Joy

Merry Christmas fills the air
With holly, spruce and pine
Bells, mistletoe, lights everywhere
Joy in your heart and mine!

Joy for family ties, friends so dear
Joy in the sharing and giving
Joy for all good Christmas cheer
Just joy in each day's living!

Best of all is a Joy so bright
Lifting Christmas day above any other
The gift of LOVE on that Holy Night
A lovely Babe and His sweet, pure Mother!

May this LOVE born long, long ago
Shine 'round you like the Christmas star
Warm you like the candle's glow
Keep Joy in your heart wherever you are!

God bless you, everyone!

The Birth of a King

As Joseph was a-walking
He heard an Angel sing
This night shall be the birth night
Of Christ, our Heavenly King.

His birth place shall be neither
In house nor in hall
Nor in the place of paradise
But in the oxen's stall.

He neither shall be washed
In white wine nor in red
But in the fair spring water
That on you shall be shed.

He neither shall be clothed
In purple nor in pall
But in the fair white linen
That is used by babies all.

He neither shall be rocked
In silver nor in gold
But in the lowly manger
That lyeth in the mold.

As Joseph was a-walking
Thus did the Angel sing
And Mary's son at midnight
Was born to be our King.

Bundles

A bundle is a funny thing
It always sets me wondering
For whether it is thin or wide
You never know just what's inside.

Especially on Christmas week
Temptation is so great to peek!
Now wouldn't it be much more fun
If shoppers carried things undone?

A Tribute to Sorors at Christmas Time

At Christmas time, Christ was born
His gift, true service to man
With love, not hate, the guide
And "Thee" not "Me," the plan.

A thousand years or more
After His holy birth
In Jersey City, eight young teachers
Lived upon this earth.

In their minds was an image
In their hearts was a glow
Of kindliness and service
To children here below.

All of us know the story
Of that glorious first year
For we were born of their vision
And so tonight we are here.

Here to be proud of our history
Of the record we've made
Of the goals we seek
Of the plans we've laid.

So we, the Eastern Region
From Alpha to Alpha Psi
Greet dear Phi Delta Kappa
And raise our voices high.

To tell her that we love her
Mother, founders, sisters true
The Eastern Region is proud
To be a part of you.

Thus the Eastern Region greets you
And humbly offers her prayer
That God will bless and keep safe
Dear Sorors everywhere.

A Babe Was Born

Christ was born
Long ago
In a lowly manger
It is so!

Shone forth a star
Holy sign!
And angels sang of Jesus
Child divine!

Humble shepherds traveled
From afar
To kneel in homage
'neath the star.

Wise men brought gifts
Rich and rare
For the Holy Infant
Lying there.

Ring out the cry
Now as then
Peace on earth, good will
To all men!

And from Bethlehem's stable
Christmas star
Peace and love shine
Where you are!

Christmas Bells

Ring out clear, O Christmas bell
As these words my ave tell
From love around the manger stall
May God's love enfold you all
And with the merry Christmas chime
Bring peace and love for all time
Let the cry ring now as then
"Peace on earth, good will to men."
Echoing o'er all the world my prayer
God bless all people everywhere.

Christmas Card

Like the candles flame of blue
Warm, dear friend, my thought for you.

So ring out, O Christmas bell
And let this rhyme my ave tell.

Like the holly and the pine
Evergreen be friendship—yours and mine!

Like rays from the shining Christmas star
Blessings on my friends, near and far.

Like the wise men's gifts of old
May the new year bring good untold.

And from the peace of the manger stall
May God's love enfold you all.

Yes, ring my ave sweet and clear
Tell my friends, Merry Christmas - A Glad New Year.

Haiku

BRIGHT Star in the sky
Shining halo for the Babe
Peace to all the earth!

Donkey – sheep – the Lamb
Christmas Star shining on high
Heralding Promise

Starlight and moonshine
Long dusty road – bed of hay
Tonight Christ is born!

Holly berry, pine
Poinsettia, shining star
Rejoice – Christ is born!

O ring bell, sing joy
Christ is born – alleluia!
Christ is born today!

For Father, on Father's Day

F is for Father, faithful year by year
A is Always Anxious to keep us free from fear
T is for Tenderness and Tending the family next
H is for Helping us to do our very best
E is for the Example by which he guides our way
R is Reliably, Resolutely, Resourcefully day by day

F-A-T-H-E-R spells Father whom we love so dear
And whose love for us is very, very clear
Though he may speak a lot or just a little bit
We are partly what we are because of it.

And whether we call you Father, Dad, or Pop
Please know we love you a whole lot
And here's a thank you from your children each and every one
We can't thank you enough for all you have done
We can only try to live our lives day by day
To make you proud of us along the way

God bless you, Pop!

CPSIA information can be obtained at www.ICGtesting.com
Printed in the USA
BVOW08s0216291215

431262BV00001B/47/P

9 781935 437956